BUS DIVORCE: SHAREHOLDER DISPUTES

A NOTEBOOK OF STRATEGIES, TACTICS AND SOLUTIONS

CLIVE TANT

All rights reserved. © Clive Tant 2018

No part of this document may be reproduced, sold, stored in or introduced into a retrieval system, or transmitted, in any form or by any means (electronic, mechanical, photocopying, recording or otherwise), without the prior permission of the copyright owner.

Disclaimer: The author assumes no responsibility for the use or misuse of this product, or for any injury, damage and/or financial loss sustained to persons or property as a direct or indirect result of using this book. The use of the information contained in this book should be based on your own due diligence, and you agree that the author is not liable for any success or failure of your business that is directly or indirectly related to the purchase and use of this information.

First printing: 2018

ISBN-13: 978-1986052498
ISBN-10: 1986052494

British Cataloguing Publication Data:
A catalogue record of this book is available from
The British Library.

Contents

Introduction 9
Part One: Understanding the Business 13
    Chapter 1-1: The Business Entity 15
        Legal Entity 15
        The Participants 16
        The Accounts, Assets and Liabilities 17
        Goodwill 18
        Customers and Other Connected Parties 19
    Chapter 1-2: Agreements Between the Business Owners 22
        Governing Documents 22
            Articles of Association 22
            Shareholders' Agreements 22
        Company Meetings and Minutes 25
        Other Commercial Agreements 26
        No Agreements! 27
    Chapter 1-3: The Business Environment 28
        The Relevant Industry, Characteristics and Protocols 28
        The Macro-economy and the Financial Success of the Business 29
Part Two: Understanding the Dispute 31
    Introduction 33

Chapter 2-1: Business Success 35
   Sale of the Century 35
   Retirement 36
   Inequality Amongst Business-Owners 38
   Different Visions 40
Chapter 2-2: Business Failure 42
   Financial Failure 42
   Inequality of Risk, Contribution or Performance 44
   Cheats and Scoundrels 45
   Greed and the Phoenix 48
Chapter 2-3: Other Influences 50
   The Lone Ranger and the Breakaway Club 50
   Interfering Third Parties 52
   That's Life 53
   The Formalities of the Relationship 54
Chapter 2-4: Relevant Law and Regulation 55
   Not a Law Book 55
   Majority Rule 56
   Directors and Their Duties 57
   Derivative Claims 58
   Remedies at Law 59
      Unfair Prejudice 59
      Just and Equitable Winding Up 60
      Other Equitable Remedies 61

    Interim Remedies 62

Part Three: Preparation 65

    Chapter 3-1: The Objective.. 67

    Chapter 3-2: The Issues and Agenda 69

        Who Owns What 69

        Who Gets What 70

        Value 72

        Who Stays and Who Goes 75

        Protections and Restrictions 76

    Chapter 3-3: War and Peace 78

        Reconciliation... 78

        Litigation 79

        Settlement 81

Part Four: Achieving the Objective................................... 85

    Chapter 4-1: Strategies.. 87

        Have a Strategy! 87

        The Good and the Bad 88

        Assessing and Understanding Respective Positions 89

            The Real Cause of Dispute 89

            Legal Merits 90

            Negotiation Strengths... 91

        Strategies for Leavers and Remainers 92

            The Minority and Outgoing Shareholders (the 'Leavers')... 92

The Majority and Remaining Shareholders (the 'Remainers') 94

Choosing a Strategy 95

Chapter 4-2: Tactics 97

Introducing Tactics 97

Advisers and Conflicts of Interests 98

Offers 99

The Legal Tools and Levers 100

Breaches and Wrongs 101

Restrictions 104

Removals and Dismissals 104

Termination and Dissolution 105

Procedural Tactics 106

Other Traps, Tricks and Tips 107

Majority Rule 107

Guarantees 107

Loan Accounts 108

Company Audit 108

Resignation as a Director 109

Employees 109

Dividends 110

Confidentiality 110

Chapter 4-3: Practical Problems and Solutions 112

Costs 112

- Taxation 114
- Share Buy-back 114
- Disposal of the Company 115
- Business Migration 116
- Chapter 4-4: Solution Vehicles 117
  - Defined Processes 117
  - Litigation 118
  - Alternative Dispute Resolution 119
    - Arbitration 119
    - Mediation 120
    - Med-Arb 121
    - Conciliation and Expert Determination 122
    - Neutral Evaluation 122
- Part Five: The Final Tips 125
- About the Author 129

Introduction

Background

This notebook is one of a small series of books written for business owners and intended to provide guidance on conflicts between owners in the same business. This particular notebook deals with private limited companies where the business owners will be shareholders who may or may not participate in the day to day running of the business.

The information in this notebook is relevant both to avoiding conflict and to dealing with it. It is intended to assist with negotiation between the conflicting parties informally, or at mediation or other alternative dispute resolution processes. It is also relevant to the formal environment of court and arbitration proceedings. The notebook offers tips and guidance which may save time, save money and save some of the inevitable hurt and agony of a Business Divorce.

Many years ago, a client likened my role to that of a family divorce lawyer. The law and the processes for resolution are quite different. Nevertheless, there are similarities in impact and outcomes. During thirty-five years in dealing with business conflicts, I have come to see the similarities in emotions and passions of both clients and their advisers.

Like a family divorce, a Business Divorce between people in business together can come about for a very wide variety of reasons. It can be dealt with formally or informally, amicably or with much hostility. It can involve a great deal of emotion and it can result in financial ruin for one or both or more parties. Very often, others than those directly involved are affected.

This is not a law book. It is a notebook which tries to weave the background of the law with the realities of business itself and of the personal and business relationships that exist. Its aim is to provide guidance on the resolution processes and to give practical rather than academic advice on achieving a resolution.

The readers

The notebook is intended to be of value to shareholders, their advisers and to those engaged in alternative dispute resolution, particularly mediators and arbitrators who might be new to disputes of this kind.

For the professional who is engaged in business disputes on a regular basis, this is not intended to be an academic work for legal reference but it is hoped that it will provide some structures, tactics and tips which may add to the reader's own knowledge and experience.

For the shareholder, it is designed to inform and, to some extent, provide comfort at what is often an uncomfortable, stressful and sometimes threatening time.

Hopefully nobody will have been misled by the title: this is not a book about family divorce. Nevertheless, if you have picked it up because you are engaged in divorce, either as an adviser or participant, and there is a company business involved then you will find that most of this work will be relevant to managing the business asset aspect of the family divorce – even if the parties decide to carry on in business together.

How to use the notebook

The notebook is divided into four major parts:

Part One – Understanding the Business

Part Two – Understanding the Dispute

Part Three – Preparation

Part Four – Achieving the Objective

The logic behind this arrangement is that you have to know what you are dealing with, understand the cause of any problem, know where you want to get to, prepare for it and then work out how to get there.

There isn't an index but the sub-sections will help the reader to dip into the notebook for particular references. If the notebook is not read from cover to cover then I encourage any adviser or shareholder engaged in a dispute to at least consider adopting the simple structure of this notebook as a strategy for managing the dispute.

> ℑ *My particular tips appear in italics and are notated by this symbol.*

Clive Tant, February 2018

Part One: Understanding the Business

Chapter 1-1: The Business Entity

Legal Entity

This notebook deals with private limited companies: that is, companies with limited liability which are owned by shareholders. It does not cover public liability companies or companies limited by guarantee, although there may be many aspects of the notebook that have a relevance particularly to public liability companies with a small number of shareholders.

It is not simply a nice point of law that the company itself is a separate 'person' in law. This has real relevance in a Business Divorce as to the continuing behaviour of shareholders, particularly if they are directors too. It also has relevance to the advice which can be provided and by whom.

Small companies in which the owners (shareholders) work and manage the business in a way similar to a partnership may be treated in certain legal situations as a quasi-partnership and the courts might be inclined to consider this when exercising discretion on appropriate remedies. So, for example, when the shareholders fall out, this might influence a decision of a court to order that a company be wound up and the proceeds distributed. The exercise of discretion in this way should not be assumed and it is wiser to ensure compliance with company law requirements and expect company law outcomes.

> *Don't make the mistake of assuming you know all about the business. Take time to find, to read and to understand anything relevant to the structure of the business.*

The Participants

Most private limited companies will have a very simple share structure. Often it will be as it was originally formed: as a company with £100 authorised share capital with 100 shares of £1 each, of which two shares have been issued. Most shareholders will know what they have but whenever there is any departure from this basic arrangement, never assume the position. The Business Divorce cannot be concluded without certainty of who owns what.

- Are there separate classes of shareholders?
- What are the class rights of separate classes?
- Are any shares held by someone as trustee for another?
- What are the terms of the trust?

> *Here are potential pitfalls for those who begin a Business Divorce without checking the rights of **everyone** involved, not just the enemy!*

Commonly, shareholders will be both directors and employees but the distinction is very important and understanding this may be fundamental to strategic and tactical decisions to be made within the Divorce.

- Are there director service contracts?
- Are they for a fixed term?
- Are there employment contracts for shareholders?

Have spouses or family members participated in the business at all? For historic tax avoidance arrangements, connected persons may have enjoyed rights and benefits whether as shareholders or otherwise and these should not be overlooked. Even if the arrangements have been entirely lawful, they might be a source of irritation in the Divorce and will need to be addressed.

> *Be particularly careful to check whether any share options might exist*

The Accounts, Assets and Liabilities

Even though most Business Divorces will be resolved ultimately with a strong element of commercial dealing, the paper evidence of the value of the business will still be material to the negotiation and even more relevant if the dispute comes before a court. The relevant date for a valuation may also be subject to argument. Do not presume that the date will be:

- The date of the last set of agreed accounts; or
- The date someone walked out; or
- The date an agreement is reached.

Be informed and be prepared to argue a case for a particular point in time by knowing:

- The history of the accounts;
- The assets which might require special valuation attention;
- What provisions for liabilities there may be and what contingent liabilities there could be which have not been provided for.

☞ *Don't leave it to the point of negotiation to mention historic issues over contribution of assets to the business, contribution to liabilities or any private or unwritten arrangements regarding benefits.*

Goodwill

This is probably the singular most emotive topic in Business Divorce negotiation. What is goodwill? Lawyers, accountants and business people will perhaps have quite different definitions but unless there is an item in the accounts then the professional advisers, professional negotiators, judges and arbitrators will be looking for an authoritative, expert valuation of the business which implicitly embraces whatever this might be.

Usually people will think in terms of the customer base and its worth and everyone involved needs to grasp that the goodwill belongs to the entity which is the company. This should influence the behaviour of directors and shareholders as the Business Divorce unravels. It is the game-playing, the interference, and the misunderstandings around this issue that usually provoke the litigation lawyers to action and the costs to soar.

If there is a figure in the accounts for goodwill, then seek out the information about the reason it's there and the value of it.

Customers and Other Connected Parties

If the customer base is the precious 'asset' of the company, then it needs protecting. The law will provide a level of protection but the cost, the time and the ultimate 'beneficiary' of litigation are usually the reasons why nothing is done and thus directors, employees and shareholders acting in bad faith often succeed in 'robbing' business from the company.

The law here is complex. As the customer base or goodwill of the business probably won't be treated as an asset of the business, any complaint against a miscreant shareholder, director or employee will most likely be wrapped up in legal claims relating to breach of duties, breach of restrictions and confidentiality. As early as possible, therefore, it is important not only to know and understand what duties and restrictions might affect individual shareholders but also to ensure that they are made aware or reminded of them. Then if a breach arises and urgent action before the courts is required, there will be a better chance of success.

As importantly, it is likely that an appropriately worded warning will be sufficient deterrent to any unlawful activity.

> *Be aware of how important this might be in any relevant litigation. It could be valuable evidence,*

so it needs to be well recorded and preserved.

The action points then are:

- Ensure that all confidential information such as the customer database is up to date, kept up to date and preserved by the company;
- Check the service and employment contracts of all those who are or might become involved in the Business Divorce and understand the restrictions;
- Understand the duties of directors (see Chapter 2-4).

Knowledge of the supply and distribution chains of a business might be as valuable as knowledge of the customer base.

- Are there contracts to be completed or honoured, either on the supply or sale side?
- Are there long-running agreements with suppliers?
- Are there distribution or agency agreements?

All this information might be useful within negotiations or in court or it might be irrelevant to the business or the dispute. Parties may be reluctant to provide information and some parties might be intimidated by obstructive responses. Nevertheless, if it is relevant then whatever hurdles there may be, efforts must be made to secure the information. It may lead to an early and disastrous conclusion if a party begins a dispute uninformed of the basic elements of the business and the share interests.

- *Non-director shareholders have limited rights to information about the business. Any director-shareholder considering resigning should therefore think twice and consider seeking advice before doing so.*

The simple principle from this chapter is:

- *Be informed; be prepared*

Chapter 1-2: Agreements Between the Business Owners

Governing Documents

Articles of Association

This document would have been part of the incorporation documents when the company was formed. All too often it is overlooked upon a presumption that it's just a list of ordinary irrelevant rules about the company. In Business Divorce there is one essential reason why this cannot be overlooked and that is to see what rights, if any, there may be regarding the pre-emption of shares – that is, the right of shareholders to acquire the shares of other shareholders.

It may not stop there because the articles may contain all manner of rules affecting the management and control of the company, including during the Divorce period, and these could be of significant strategic and tactical value. For example, they may be relevant to the removal of a director.

Shareholders' Agreements

Such agreements can be valuable to an early resolution of a Divorce but as with any legal document the success of this might depend on how well written the document may be.

A professionally written document might be very wide-ranging whereas sometimes there might be a single issue which the shareholders have decided to record. One dangerous circumstance is where a shareholder agreement is used for a single purpose and without sufficient regard to other circumstances that might be or become relevant. This can often be the case where shareholder agreements are entered into as part of 'key man' insurance policies.

However, a shareholders' agreement may become *too* complex to draft and implement if shareholders fully anticipate the retirement or death of one of them and consider:

- What should happen to the outgoing shareholder's shares;
- Whether any successor should be entitled to be a director also;
- Whether there should be dividend protection for the successor shareholder;
- Whether there should be any change in voting rights and/or additional protection for successor minorities.

The retirement or death of a shareholder might seem to be a different circumstance to a Business Divorce but such events very often trigger disputes for a variety of reasons. Thus, some prior consideration of the items listed above may help to minimise the scope for dispute.

Prior agreement on such matters is difficult because of the unlikelihood that all shareholders will have the same personal circumstances and so find it easy to reach agreement on shareholder rights after retirement or death.

More likely and as valuable will be a provision for termination of the shareholder agreement in defined circumstances and this will usually be combined with a defined process for share purchase of one or more share interests. These may range from a simple valuation by the accountant to the business to more complex negotiation structures which have an in-built protection against compulsory share sale or purchase at low or inflated prices.

Similarly, many shareholder agreements may contemplate a business sale and impose compulsory sale arrangements ('tag along/drag along') to protect shareholders and ensure they too can benefit from a sale (tag along rights) or to compel shareholders to sell their interests in certain circumstances (drag along rights).

However, what these provisions cannot easily contemplate is the commercial position of the company and the financial standing of the shareholders at the time when they may become relevant. This often gives rise to an abuse of a defined process by shareholders who may be in a dominant financial position. Such 'abuse' may have an element of moral irresponsibility but if there is compliance with an agreed process within an enforceable shareholders' agreement then the 'abused' party may find it difficult to rely upon the sympathy of the law.

Thus, a simple provision which ensures equality of reward (by dividends, income etc) amongst working shareholders may be a fatal burden to the business if the shareholders have not made adequate financial provision for the impact of the death or critical illness of shareholders whose efforts determine the profitability of the business. To avoid this, the agreement needs to deal adequately with termination of the agreement and perhaps compulsory share purchase.

> *If a shareholders' agreement is created either at the outset of the business, during its lifetime or as a solution to a dispute between shareholders there must be regard to the commerciality of the provisions. Failure to do so probably will not render the provision unenforceable but may ironically create an unfairness albeit different to the mischief it was designed to overcome.* ***A balance of vision and pragmatism is required.***

Company Meetings and Minutes

The '*ivory tower*' world of the lawyers comes to life when a judge asks parties where the written record is of something they have agreed. It's simply a matter of evidence but usually it's evidence of a quality that makes it easier for a judge to determine the credibility of one side or the other.

Even a short email or a scrap of paper referencing an agreement on a particular issue between shareholders may be good evidence, and good evidence can carry weight across a negotiating table or at a mediation almost as much as it might inside a court room.

> *Always think what evidence there may be to corroborate an argument, even if there is little prospect of it being needed in a court room.*

Other Commercial Agreements

All too often, in the throes of finalising a Business Divorce settlement one party will recall an element of history when the parties agreed some particular item or issue. The late introduction of fundamental issues by design as an ambush or even in innocence is rarely conducive to settlement. To avoid the situation, parties really must give good examination of their memories and of any other documents that might have a relevance to the Divorce, either directly or indirectly, perhaps as a ramification of the Divorce itself. For example:

- Are there any share option agreements or charges upon the shares?
- Are there personal guarantees to be cleared?
- Are there commercial agreements with provisions for termination if there is a change of control of the business?
- Are there key man or insurance policies which will come to an end or which need to be provided for in some way?
- Are there any assets which sit outside the company but are relevant to the business and are jointly owned by the shareholders?

☞ *Do not regard such matters as purely administrative.*

No Agreements!

Perhaps the most common situation is that there are no relevant agreements at all and the governing documents of the company, the articles and memorandum of association are in a standard form without relevance to the Business Divorce.

How then do the parties get their Divorce? Without prior agreement between shareholders as to the circumstances in which their relationship may come to an end, they are left with having to rely upon underlying law that governs the management of companies and its shareholders (essentially the Companies Acts) or provides for remedies or relief for fractious shareholders (the Insolvency Act 1986 and again the Companies Acts and their Regulations). The alternative, of course, is that parties simply negotiate and achieve a consensus. Often it is when consensus cannot be reached, when one or more parties employs commercial leverage, strategic and tactical game-playing or just bullying, that the relationship deteriorates, the business suffers and the parties spend money with lawyers.

Very much the reasoning behind this notebook is that in such circumstances, the parties will at least be aware of what is happening and so be able to control the situation better.

Chapter 1-3: The Business Environment

The Relevant Industry, Characteristics and Protocols

A Business Divorce cannot be managed in isolation to the environment in which the business operates. It is not only the parties in dispute who must be mindful of this but also the professional advisers and the resolvers: that is, the mediators, arbitrators and judges. It is a dispute between shareholders which will be at the heart of the Business Divorce but the business itself belongs to the company. Unless the business itself is facing termination then the company can expect the business to continue and any resolution or judgment should be made with that in mind.

This might require consideration of a range of characteristics that might be particular to the industry or business. Licensing, qualification and regulation may all be 'controls' on the conduct of the business that might impact on the ability of the company to perform successfully or at all. Where these rights and other resources and skills reside might be relevant for the performance of the business, to the value of the business and the share interests in it.

> *Ensure that any adviser and any resolver or facilitator has a grasp of the business and its environment before they engage in a Business Divorce process.*

The Macro-economy and the Financial Success of the Business

When the economy is in good shape and businesses generally are doing well, Business Divorces may be less frequent. Also, when the company's business itself is financially successful, the shareholders find it easier to accept the weaknesses of their business-owning colleagues. It is when times are not so good that shareholders will look more introspectively at the performance and contribution others are making to the success of the business.

A valuer of the business or of a share interest will look at a point in time with reference to the recorded financial performance of the business and with some regard to forecast performance. The expert valuer, however, is not the entrepreneur and the entrepreneur (shareholder) should not be timid in challenging the expert. Nevertheless, if a party in dispute wants the other side to have regard to his/her visions and judgments then they must be made known and it is better that they have the credibility of expert support.

> *The parties should set out clearly their vison of the future if they expect that to be a consideration in the negotiation or determination of the dispute.*

Part Two: Understanding the Dispute

Introduction

There are very many reasons why a Business Divorce may come about and for there to be a successful outcome it is essential that the parties involved and their advisers really understand why there is a dispute.

Of course, there are many circumstances where business participants agree to part company or close a business with complete amicability but like many marital divorces, the squabbling might only start when the time comes to divide the spoils of the relationship.

The reasons why participants may not be wanting to continue in business together are not necessarily the same as the reasons behind a dispute. The retirement of a founding shareholder might have been long anticipated by all but when it comes to it happening the dispute may be about his/her succession, either in management or shareholding or both.

Behaviour and appearances can be relevant. If one side to a dispute considers the other side is being greedy then there must be a mirror view which considers how the position is viewed from the other side. It is inadequate simply to see the other party as greedy. If a solution is to be found then it is important to try and ascertain what drives the 'greed' and sometimes to work out the 'needs' and not simply the 'wants' behind the perceived greed.

> *It is fundamental to everyone involved, whether as*

parties or advisers, that every effort is made to understand the other side's position to the fullest extent possible. Solutions often lie in what is behind the stated position.

Chapter 2-1: Business Success

Sale of the Century

The dream of many shareholders will be to take their business to a point of success where it becomes the target for a predator business willing to pay handsomely for the shareholding. Whether by chance or by design, a prospective purchaser may come along offering the riches that one or more of the shareholders might have been wishing for. The joy of the shareholders is often muted when the detail of the purchase terms is negotiated.

- It is now perhaps the norm for there to be an element of deferred consideration.
- It is also common for the purchaser to require key personnel to remain in the business for a defined period.
- The key personnel may include one but not all of the shareholders.
- Restrictive covenants will almost certainly be required by a purchaser.

These may prompt disputes because the personal circumstances of outgoing shareholders are likely to be different. Their ages, retirement plans and financial circumstances may all lead to the shareholders wanting something different from a sale – even a good sale.

> *Before the shareholders get too deeply in dispute about a sale, make sure that a sale to an identifiable*

> *prospective purchaser is a serious prospect.*

A well written shareholders' agreement might anticipate issues between shareholders at the time of sale and contain 'drag along' or 'tag along' rights and obligations (see Chapter 1-2). Even then, it isn't the best of circumstances if one or more of the shareholders is being compelled to accept a position against their choosing and disruptive, non-co-operative shareholders might jeopardise that sale of the century.

> ☥ *If a sale can be anticipated, get all the shareholders on board before the negotiations with the purchaser begin.*

Retirement

Different life ambitions and expectations are likely to apply to shareholders who contribute time to a business. Their retirement plans will usually be far more varied and flexible than someone in paid employment without a business interest.

Again, a distinction needs to be made between the roles of employees and shareholders. Compulsory retirement was an easy solution for many businesses until the Employment Equality (Age) Regulations 2006 introduced a level of uncertainty for those business people not employed and significant protection for those who are.

A shareholders' agreement could provide for a compulsory

transfer of shares at a certain age but I have never seen one that does! This is in contrast to many professional partnership arrangements.

What is it that retiring shareholders want?

- Is it a sale of the shareholding to provide capital for retirement?
- Is it simply to stop working but to retain a shareholding?
- Do they need an income stream from dividends?
- If they retain a shareholding, do they still want to be a director?
- Will the shares continue to have the same voting power?

And an even bigger question – do they want their chosen successor to replace them?

Shareholder agreements really should deal with these questions and in the mid-nineties, when shareholder agreements became vogue, I produced a matrix to prompt shareholders to think about these questions, to discuss the issues and so reach agreement. The reality was that the issues are so fraught with options that clients never could agree.

That isn't to say that the issues can or should be ignored or left until they arise. Simple solutions might be the answer but it does mean that the shareholders then elect to play a poker game where a party with the best hand or the biggest pot or the best health/mental capacity might clean up!

- *In preparing for the future, don't ignore these issues.*

- *If retirement possibilities are already being discussed, think broadly about these issues, not simply as problems but also as solutions.*

If a solution cannot be found that accommodates the wishes of both those who wish to retire and those who wish to stay, then the ultimate solution might be an application to the court for there to be a just and equitable winding up of the business (see Chapter 2-4). Of course, the shareholders of a solvent business may agree that there be a voluntary winding up with a realisation of the assets and a distribution but whether the parties agree it or a court orders it, it is likely there will be significantly less in the pot to distribute.

- *Whether retiring or staying on, don't be stubborn in this situation. It is more likely than not there will be a solution which will accommodate both positions. The alternative will not!*

Inequality Amongst Business-Owners

Rarely can it be true when two or more shareholders describe themselves as 'equal'. In what respect? They may have equality of shareholding and income but it is unlikely that they will have equality of influence within the company.

The sales director may have the control of the customer base; the technical director may have control and knowledge of the processes and another director may have the support of the staff. In law this shouldn't be a problem, particularly when the duties of directors *to the company* are considered, but by the time lawyers get involved to protect the company, the damage is usually done, either in the marketplace or to the competitive position or to the workforce.

So much business success has to be achieved on the back of trust but it is when shareholders perceive inequality of contribution and reward that trust begins to fail, selfishness or self-preservation creep in and Business Divorce is on the cards. (See Chapter 2-2 below on Business Failure for a more detailed consideration of these circumstances).

Again, a good shareholders' agreement will address the monitoring of contribution and reward and provide for additional levels of security for the business. Alongside should be a well-drafted service agreement for the directors, perhaps tailored to their situation.

> *Does the shareholders' agreement have covenants which the shareholders might enforce personally against one another and which the company may enforce? This makes for tighter protection and avoids having to rely upon derivative actions being brought in the name of the company (see Chapters 2-4 and 4-2).*

The inequality may be simply an inequality of shareholding

and usually for so long as the business is successful and everyone is *happily* enjoying the spoils of success, that inequality will be of little consequence.

However, success is often the result of a primary attribute – the product design, or a sales campaign or initiative, or one individual's skills or efforts. Often the reward for individuals is provided by or enhanced by a share interest. I have regularly questioned whether this is necessary or the best way of maintaining success.

- *There is nearly always another way to reward individual achievement than to disturb shareholder balances and the status quo. It may not be too late to find an alternative and so avoid the Business Divorce.*

- *If that has happened and the Business Divorce occurs, always examine the circumstances of the additional allocation, its correctness in law (the articles of association, shareholders' agreement) and consider its basic correctness as a matter of contract.*

Different Visions

As with life itself, business is dynamic and the dreams, expectations and ambitions of the original business and early years might change as the business, its products or services, its personnel and the personal interests of the shareholders change and develop. Failure to agree to move in a particular direction is not uncommon and Business Divorce is often a consequence.

If the business is such that it can be divided and if the shareholders can find a solution to deal with any inequality of division then that might be the cheapest and best solution for all. Often that is the case where there is a customer base that can be divided and the respective parties each have the resources to manage a new business. It is rarely the most sensible solution for the business to be simply broken up and assets realised but it is often the consequence if the shareholders cannot agree another solution. As with a retirement, it is more likely than not that there will be a solution which will accommodate both positions.

> *If parties Divorce because of different visions, there should be transparency between them about intentions going forward and protection for all by way of mutual cross covenants.*

Chapter 2-2: Business Failure

Financial Failure

Perhaps surprisingly, I believe that this is ***not*** the most common reason for a Business Divorce. Financial failure of a business is more akin to death than divorce. Good solutions for all shareholders are rarely available and often it is personal survival that might provoke a dispute over liabilities rather than salvaging what might be left.

If the business hasn't died but is very sick and capable of full or partial recovery, then that is a different circumstance. There is then the equivalent of the matrimonial home, the savings and the debts to fight over. If the paper/accounts value of the business is poor, then there is perhaps more scope for dispute. A low net asset value or low EBITDA (see Chapter 3-2) will likely mean that no one will be interested in purchasing the business, including any of the shareholders. There is then wide scope for tactical play:

- The leverage of legal threats is low: who will spend money with lawyers pursuing something that isn't worth it?
- The shareholders with the greater control on 'survivable assets' have a better position: the sales director/shareholder with the personal customer contacts; the technology director/shareholder with the know-how.
- The potential weakness of directors/shareholders who have significant loan accounts – whether they

are loans to or from the company!

☞ *Understanding these positions and levers is essential for a negotiation between shareholders divorcing when there is still something to salvage but the bargaining positions are seemingly unequal.*

Whose fault is it? What does it matter? In all probability, as with 'no fault divorce', it won't matter at all. It may well be that there has been some breach of duty by a director/shareholder or that one or more director/shareholder has acted without capacity or authority and may even have gained personally. The biggest problem a complaining shareholder has is that of identifying and accepting that the primary loss is likely to be that of the company itself, leaving the affected shareholder without a direct remedy or without much of a threat at a negotiation (see Chapter 2-4 on Derivative Claims).

This is often so in the most blatant and unfair of situations:

- The managing director/shareholder who has overspent on the company car;
- The sales director/shareholder who has abused entertainment allowances;
- The directors/shareholders who have benefited from extraordinary pension contributions.

It isn't a case that the law is without a remedy for acts or omissions of real abuse but often the solutions take time and money and produce little benefit early enough to be of value in the negotiations for the Business Divorce settlement.

> *Parties in a Business Divorce must be real with their expectations as to what wrongs can be remedied, what it costs to secure a remedy and what the net worth may be.*

> *It's usually too late by the time the Business Divorce comes around but the answer to protecting the real worth in a business and preventing it being hi-jacked by one party at any time – and particularly at a time of financial difficulty – is to protect key assets by having a company structure that removes those assets, such as land and intellectual property, to ownership in a separate legal entity.*

Inequality of Risk, Contribution or Performance

When times are good, shareholders, particularly the working director/shareholders, worry less or not at all if there is inequality with other director/shareholders, for example:

- Where not all of the director/shareholders may have signed a personal guarantee for the bank overdraft or the factoring arrangement; or
- Where one director/shareholder may have provided less working capital when the business was started; or

- Where one director/shareholder may not be working the same hours as the other directors/shareholders.

Of course, when the sales are falling off, or margins are reduced if someone's personal financial position begins to look unfairly better than the rest at times when the business is struggling, then these matters do become important – or seemingly so!

Without being addressed, if such kinds of issues fester to the point where Business Divorce is likely, what is to be done? Most obviously the inequality should be addressed but it firstly needs to be recognised and accepted as an inequality. If the parties cannot do this themselves can it be achieved by third party intervention or determination? The shareholders will need to 'sign up' to a method that provides or seeks to provide a solution. It may be that in a shareholders' agreement there is a provision for a dispute resolution process. If there isn't, it doesn't stop the parties agreeing to one.

> *If a new resolution process is agreed or if a solution is found with or without a process, ensure that there is 'valuable consideration' for the solution, otherwise it may be unenforceable.*

Cheats and Scoundrels

Shareholders don't usually begin their shareholding life intending to cheat other shareholders or to behave in a mischievous way for their own selfish benefit and very often they are not cheats and scoundrels even though they may be accused of being such by other shareholders.

Nevertheless, it happens that shareholders will try to take advantage of others, thus triggering allegations of cheating or simply unfairness (akin sometimes to adultery or unreasonable behaviour of individuals) and often leading to demands for a Business Divorce. The truth is that it's often easier to get out of a marriage than it might be for a shareholder to remove himself or herself as a shareholder *and* to recover the right value of the shareholding.

If there is one tactic that cheats and scoundrels rely upon and if there is one obstacle the afflicted shareholders struggle with, it is the principle of majority rule. Holding a majority shareholding may be over-used and used to abuse a minority but all shareholders have to accept that this is a cardinal principle of English company law. Only in exceptional situations will the courts intervene and despite a wealth of case law it is difficult to identify, list or define what those situations might be (see Chapter 2-4).

> *Do not confuse the exercise of the will of the majority of shareholders in general meetings with the exercise of the powers and duties of the directors.*

It is important therefore to carefully consider the actions of shareholders, particularly within the content and context of any shareholders' agreement, the articles of association and the Companies Acts and Regulations before judgments are made as to the lawfulness of acts or omissions of which the shareholders may be accused. If the judgment is that the act or omission is lawful but unfair and prejudicial to other shareholders, then the 'injured' shareholders might have a remedy (see Chapter 2-4).

However, if the act or omission is wrong then there must be consideration as to who has the legal standing to do something about it. This usually focuses upon who suffers as a result and the common error of 'injured' shareholders is to believe that the loss is theirs when in fact the loss is, at least prima facie, that of the company. It is the company that suffers a loss because of unjustified or unapproved remuneration, pension contributions or expenditure reimbursement/allowances of director shareholders. Of course, this can impact upon the value of the injured shareholders' interests in the company and it may be unfair and/or prejudicial but it is the company that suffers the primary loss and has the better claim against the miscreant director/shareholders.

With the wrongs having been committed or omitted by directors/shareholders with majority control of the company, no action against them will ever be authorised in the name of the company and it is in this situation that the injured shareholders may apply to the court to bring a derivative claim in the name of the company (see Chapter 2-4).

> *Directors' duties are owed to the company and not to the shareholders and so the best foundation for a claim by shareholders against other shareholders*

is usually a breach of the shareholders' agreement.

Greed and the Phoenix

Shareholders may be accused of being greedy at times of business failure as much as when the business is successful. Often this will be at a time when, even if the company is solvent, its future failure appears obvious. The temptation to get out of the company "what you can" is a common attitude and often this might be achieved with professional assistance, albeit proper and lawful, which will commonly see the demise of a business and its resurrection but perhaps without all of the previous shareholders involved.

A new 'investor' may insist upon the exclusion of one or more shareholders in any venture going forward or the failure of the company might be seen as a simple way of ditching an unwanted business associate.

Such plans are often accompanied by various breaches of duty by director/shareholders including the migration of business to parallel companies, secret agreements with customers, deliberate concealment of business information etc., all of which might be of such desperate importance to the company or the other shareholders as to justify some urgent action (see Chapter 2-4 Interim Remedies).

At such times it is fundamental to have a level-headed commercial analysis of the business going forward, whether that is the existing business or a scaled down operation by the injured shareholders, as well as an analysis of the costs, costs recovery and benefit of any court proceedings.

3 *The director/shareholders who look to benefit, as against other shareholders, from the failure of the company will be expecting it to be removed from the Companies Register – and usually for this to happen as a matter of routine. For so long as the company remains registered they may remain exposed to claims by the company, its liquidators and its creditors. Thus, the 'injured' shareholders should ensure that notification is given to Companies House requesting that the company not be removed.*

Chapter 2-3: Other Influences

The Lone Ranger and the Breakaway Club

"Sometimes people are just not meant for one another." So it is often said when marriages fail and so it is in business as well. When the participants are only two in number then the relationship may not last long as their divergent ambitions, visions and expectations are soon exposed. When there are more than two, it is easier for these characteristics to be concealed. That may be more so as a business grows and other participants are recruited. Then there is the danger that one or more participants with other ideas starts to develop a desire to "do their own thing".

A real difficulty arises when the Lone Ranger or the Breakaway Club are simply shareholders and neither directors nor employees. Without a contractual provision in a shareholders' agreement then, as shareholders only, they have no legal duty of loyalty. As employees and more so as directors, they have duties to observe. There may also be additional restraints within service contracts or shareholders agreements. Also, there may be other legal protections for the business itself in the laws that might protect assets, particularly intellectual property rights, including the protection of databases and property.

However, the reality is that when one or more of the participants are set on a different path, the probability is that a Business Divorce will happen. The disaffected participants may become mischievous and turn into cheats and scoundrels (see Chapter 2-2). Rather than having to deal with the disaffection by manipulation of the situation (on the part of the disaffected) or treating it as mutiny (in the eyes of those not disaffected), the participants should grasp the nettle of reality early and ... talk.

How ridiculous a strategy is this? Well, if the reality is that one or more participants are going to leave then both 'sides' need to address the process and the consequences of that at the start. If the disaffected think that transparency is commercially suicidal, this needs to be weighed against the risk of acting surreptitiously and committing a legal wrong or, even if no wrong is committed, being accused of doing so. This is feeding frenzy time for the lawyers!

Whatever legal restraints might be in place, whatever real issues there may be over share interests and values and whatever commercial awkwardness there might be, it is most likely to be cheaper, quicker and less acrimonious if the parties can be transparent with one another. If they cannot reach a solution easily then they could look to a resolution procedure to help reach agreement. Mediation is the most likely forum for this but if it simply comes down to a valuation of a share interest then the parties might consider appointing a valuer for expert determination.

Of course, the early discussion of an issue before it festers might not only avoid a lot of acrimony and cost. It could uncover a simple misunderstanding. Poor communication is often at the very heart of commercial disputes – of all kinds.

3   *Acknowledging that a relationship is at an end and*

discussing it openly isn't naivety.

Interfering Third Parties

What happens when the sales director/shareholder is offered a bounty by a competitor? All that is written above about greed, cheats and breakaway factions could become relevant. The same logic, approach and principles apply. There might be protections for the business and the other shareholders. There might seem to be a danger in the sales director letting it be known that a golden egg awaits him but are there really downsides for either party in discussing the situation? It is only if one party wishes to be mischievous and probably do something wrongful or unlawful (not necessarily criminal) that there can be any good tactical consideration of secrecy and stealth.

Of course, the interfering third parties may place themselves at risk by encouraging a breakaway. If that is potentially unlawful then they could be warned off their interference by a suitable notice from the company or the remaining shareholders, depending on the nature of the unlawfulness.

> ༣ *BIG TIP It is often a very strong legal tactical move to be open with the other side even if, usually in desperation, one party decides it must act wrongfully. To be able to evidence the openness of an action before a court can be of real value.*

That's Life

The two certainties in life – that is, death and taxation – have a relevance to business as well. Unlike shares held by a corporate entity or a trust, a shareholding by an individual cannot continue forever. If a shareholder wants a family interest in a business to continue after his or her death, then they need to consider moving ownership of the shares before death or upon death and doing so in a way which is always compliant with the law of the land and the rules of the company.

The personal interest in the business for private limited companies isn't usually limited to the shares. A right to sit in the boardroom is often regarded as concomitant with a shareholding. That might not be the view of the directors who never did like the widow of their recently departed managing director! He, on the other hand, always thought that she knew the business as well as he did and would be an ideal replacement. What do the articles of association provide for? Is there a shareholders' agreement which deals with the point? If the answer isn't already provided for, how will the parties resolve the position? Again, the principle of discussion and, if necessary, alternative dispute resolution – perhaps conciliation or mediation – must be the better approach than doing nothing and waiting for litigation.

> *Shame on shareholders to allow this situation to arise. It isn't easy to reconcile personal, individual and family interests (see Chapter 1-2) and to reach agreement before the event arises but there is a moral responsibility to try.*

The Formalities of the Relationship

As mentioned in Chapter 1-2, there must be an examination of the documents that govern the shareholders' relationship, such as the articles of association and shareholders' agreement. That examination is a pre-requisite to understanding and managing a Business Divorce. As indicated in this Part and in Part Four, there may be situations where one party might want to ignore or overlook the formalities of the relationship as provided by the governing documents and the relevant law (see Chapter 2-4), but that does not mean that the formalities can be altogether disregarded. A misjudgement or poor advice on the strategy, tactics and relative bargaining positions could lead to disaster if the formal and legal position has not been considered.

> *No matter what strength of bargaining position one party may have, it is simply dangerous to assume that such strength will prevail against the law.*

Chapter 2-4: Relevant Law and Regulation

Not a Law Book

As mentioned in the introduction, this notebook has not been written as a law book but a Business Divorce cannot be managed with disregard to what the law is and, in particular, to what legal remedies and solutions there may be.

Of course, with appropriate consensus, shareholders who no longer wish to participate in business together may agree how their separation is to be dealt with. That separation must still be lawful and legally effective. It may often be as simple as one party purchasing the shares of another by paying the price and receiving the shares. That is unlikely to be the situation with someone who has chosen to pick up and read this notebook!

To write about all the relevant law and regulation in any detail would be to write a law book. The readers and their advisers may well require a law book alongside but at the least, all readers should be mindful that the Companies Act 2006 is the underlying statute for the conduct and governance of limited liability companies. To this statutory reference bedrock must be added the layer of common law that has a particular relevance to the rulings of the courts in shareholder and company disputes as well as a layer of regulation: not only secondary legislation, which relates to companies in general, but to regulation that might be particular to the business, the industry or the profession in which the business trades.

Thus, this chapter is limited to the most relevant of legal principles that might impact upon the conduct of a Business Divorce.

Majority Rule

The principle of majority rule is readily understood and accepted by all but, in the context of a Business Divorce, one must be mindful of situations where the basic principle may need a deeper understanding.

A more sophisticated arrangement between shareholders may, for example, have a share structure with different classes of shares with different rights, particularly voting rights. In certain circumstances a shareholders' agreement or the articles of association might provide that particular shares or votes might be weighted. So, for example, upon an effective 'expulsion' of a shareholder compelled to leave the business and to sell his shares, the target shareholder may be entitled to enhanced voting rights.

The courts must be expected to staunchly uphold majority rule as a cardinal principle of company law. That does not mean that in all circumstances the holders of more than fifty per cent of the voting rights can do just as they please. It is this common mistake that usually leads to the bullying of a minority by the majority and one which will give the minority the argument of unfairly prejudicial treatment and the right to go to court for a remedy (see Unfair Prejudice below).

There may also be situations when a simple majority is not enough, whether by statutory provision or as may be agreed between shareholders. Thus, by s84 Insolvency Act 1986, a special resolution requiring a majority of 75% of the members entitled to vote is required to pass a resolution to wind up the company. This is perhaps the best example relevant to the tactics that might be employed in Business Divorce negotiations, which illustrates the danger of assuming that shareholders with a simple majority may always do as they please.

Directors and Their Duties

In a Business Divorce, shareholders who are not directors may have to accept some limitation to their strength and negotiating position. The shareholders vest the management of the business in the board of directors and even though the shareholders may control the composition of the board and may have some power in general meetings of the company, a minority shareholder without voting power in a general meeting and not himself/herself a director may be at a disadvantage within a Business Divorce process.

Careful attention should be paid to the rights and powers of directors as may be provided by the articles of association, shareholders' agreement or any service agreement a director may have. The power of directors to issue shares may, for example, be a powerful tactical weapon in the dispute.

However, the directors are in a fiduciary position and owe fiduciary duties to the company (although not in general to the shareholders). Sections 170 – 181 of the Companies Act 2006 essentially codified the previously common law duties of acting honestly, with good faith, properly exercising powers and avoiding conflicts of interest. The statute does allow, however, a director to act where he/she may have an interest in a transaction or arrangement entered into by the company, subject to appropriate disclosure (s182 Companies Act 2006). Also, where a director has transgressed, there *may* be an escape route by the company, i.e., the members, ratifying the director's acts that might amount to negligence, default, breach of duty or breach of trust (s239 Companies Act 2006).

> *Before the Business Divorce gets underway, review what the directors have done and whether all is in order.*

Derivative Claims

If the concept that the company is a separate legal person is grasped, then it is easier to understand that when a wrong is done to the company, it is the company, not the shareholders, that has the right to bring an action. What is more, although there may be a residual power with the company in general meetings, as the management of the company lies with the directors, it is they who may decide whether or not to do anything.

This often leaves minority shareholders feeling helpless if

they have no board presence or no voting influence at board or general meeting level. With significant complexity as to the circumstances in which it can be used, there is provision (sections 260-269 Companies Act 2006) for a shareholder to obtain permission from the court to bring a derivative claim in the name of the company for a wrong done to the company. This is one potential weapon in the armoury of combatants in a Business Divorce which is most likely to require careful consideration by lawyers before it is even threatened to be launched.

> *Do not confuse wrongs done to the company with wrongs to the shareholders.*

Remedies at Law

There are two fundamental statutory remedies available that may protect shareholders:

- A claim based upon an argument of **unfair prejudice** to a shareholder's position;
- An application that the company be wound up on the grounds that it is **just and equitable** to do so.

Unfair Prejudice

Perhaps the most likely route taken by shareholders who feel aggrieved, who want out of the company and who feel that their shareholding is otherwise imprisoned, is to argue that they have a cause of action to bring a claim under s994 of the Companies Act 2006. The remedy usually sought is an order that the other shareholder(s) be compelled to purchase the complainant's shares.

Fundamentally, a shareholder must establish that the actions complained of are ***both*** unfair *and* prejudicial. The court will have a discretion as to what the remedy should be if a case is established.

So much of Business Divorce between shareholders is conducted against a backdrop and threat of an application of this kind being made that much of the content of this notebook can be applied to such a situation. In reality, for so many shareholders the cost of funding a dispute on this premise is so expensive that the threat is hollow. That is not to say that the 'accused' shareholder(s) – or defendants, as they would become – may always ignore the threat. The risk that a case is brought and succeeds with the inherent risk of the court award and probably two legal bills to pay must be considered.

Just and Equitable Winding Up

An often-ignored alternative for a complainant shareholder is to threaten an application under s122(1)(g) of the Insolvency Act 1986. For the purpose of this notebook, if not as a matter of law, it can be said that there is fundamentally little difference between the grounds for either a section 994 petition or a petition under section 122. There are other differences, however, and perhaps the most fundamental and relevant is that for section 122 petition; there is a necessity to demonstrate that there is a tangible interest or resultant value in there being a winding up of the company.

It is a more targeted and draconian remedy. For that reason, the threat may be more effective but because of this the court will look carefully at the integrity or misuse of such an application. The court itself might decline to make an order if it is felt that justice can be done by ordering some other remedy, which may in fact be an order to purchase shares, but as that is not the basis of making such an application, the petitioner might want to reflect and be careful of what he/she may wish for.

Other Equitable Remedies

Court remedies, particularly for minority shareholders, are not limited to the statutory remedies. The courts might be willing to intervene and 'grant relief' on principles of equity. Thus, the courts may intervene in circumstances where:

- The majority shareholders abuse their power by waiving or ratifying a breach of duty to the company (this is the foundation of the derivative action, which is an exception to the cardinal principle of majority rule);
- The majority vote to change the articles of association to undermine the minority;
- There may exist a fiduciary duty *between* shareholders;
- There is a quasi-partnership arrangement and where the majority exercises its power perhaps beyond

what the parties may ever have contemplated.

These remedies largely overlap the statutory remedies. Their suitability and applicability usually involve serious and detailed legal consideration and, because they involve the exercise of a court's discretion outside of the statutory arena, there will always be less certainty as to the outcome.

It is wise therefore to be aware that legal solutions in a Business Divorce might not be limited to the two statutory remedies. Nevertheless, an applicant must be mindful that, where a party might have a plausible explanation for its actions or omissions, seeking a determination from the court may not be the easiest, the quickest or the cheapest solution.

> *Using the legal process as a tool of negotiation comes with a cost and a risk which must be entirely understood and accepted before action is commenced.*

Interim Remedies

Of course, there may be situations that are critical to the business or the position of a party to the Business Divorce where an urgent application to the court for an interim solution (as the lawyers will say - "interlocutory relief") by way of an injunction (an order to do or not to do something) or even the appointment of a receiver (s37 Supreme Court Act 1981) might be necessary. This is a subject deserving of a notebook in itself, even for the layman, and for the purposes of this notebook it is best to highlight and to summarise just the key factors that will be relevant to the consideration of the lawyers and to the court:

- This is another area where the court's discretion is exercised;
- It is essential that the party seeking an injunction be able to show that it has an arguable case;
- Then the party must show that it has an interest to protect and that the balance of convenience lies in favour of an injunction being granted;
- It could be that an award of damages (meaning loosely 'compensation') might be an adequate remedy and so displace the necessity for an injunction.

3 *Avoid becoming involved in interlocutory litigation processes unless it is really necessary. They are costly and usually do not provide or lead to early solutions unless one party becomes intimidated by the cost and the process.*

Part Three:
Preparation

Chapter 3-1: The Objective

I have always been insistent on the objective being identified at the very beginning. Does the aggrieved owner want to stay or go, remain as an owner but abandon all other involvement, oust the other owner(s) or achieve a realisation of the business for all? Will there be competition between rival businesses going forward or is this to be 'bought off'? Does an aggrieved or outgoing owner simply want a quiet departure and an easy retirement? Is revenge or recompense of importance?

Very often the owner doesn't have a clear idea as to what he/she wants and sometimes they need advice about what they can achieve but that is not an excuse for not determining the objective. Without a defined objective, the way ahead can simply become confused, unsuccessful and expensive. It is also important to understand the monetary *worth* or other relevant *value* of a defined objective to avoid straying into skirmishes which are likely to achieve little more than to increase costs.

Try and assess the position as realistically as possible at the start, no matter how hard that may be to do or to deal with. At some stage during a dispute process both sides should be confronted by a reality check, whether that is brought about by a mediator, the adviser or the other side. Most of all, avoid that reality check being delivered at the end by a judge!

> ༣ *Don't begin to commence a Business Divorce or to*

engage with the other side until the objective of the divorce has been determined.

3 *From the start, be clear and realistic about the outcome.*

Having set the objective and before deciding how to achieve the objective, it is sensible to analyse where there might be consensus, where there will be disagreement and, as part of an early reality check of the objective itself, which arguments can be won and which might be hopeless.

Chapter 3-2: The Issues and Agenda

Who Owns What

All too often, shareholders in small and medium size enterprise companies fail to grasp that their ownership interest in the company is an interest in the shares themselves and, most usually, only the shares. It may be that the company may have started business life as a partnership and then converted to a company, with the partnership assets being hived up to the company in exchange for shares, and it may be that the participants still behave as partners such that the lawyers will describe the enterprise as a quasi-partnership (see Chapter 1-1).

Nevertheless, as shareholders, the participants own shares – a share of the company. It is the company that owns all the assets, just as the company is responsible for the liabilities, not the shareholders. Nevertheless, shareholders commonly talk about and believe that: the company car belongs to them; the company pension fund is their pension fund; the customers they have introduced *belong* to them; the assets they introduced to start the business still belong to them; the premises are owned by all the shareholders; the intellectual property of the company belongs to them because it was their idea, and so on.

Of course, many shareholders are not naïve, and many may have taken appropriate steps to separate the identity of assets they genuinely and legally own from the assets of the company. In many cases shareholders would have been advised to separate the ownership of some or all assets so that those of monetary or commercial value are not at risk in the event of the business failing because of insolvency. A separate company or partnership might be used to own assets such as property and intellectual property rights.

What of the shares themselves? Are the shareholders clear as to what shares they own? Are there separate classes of shares with separate rights and separate interests? What are they? In particular, what are the voting rights attached to the shares?

The enquiry and analysis into who owns what must be undertaken at the start.

> *Like setting the objective, it isn't sensible to engage with the other shareholders until these ownership issues are clear.*

Who Gets What

It might be thought that who gets what is determined by a simple choice of process: the parties either negotiate successfully and settle, or fail to settle, and, ultimately, a third party, probably a judge, will decide. Generally, that will be so but in many situations the scope for tactical play may mean long delays in either process being started. The relationship festers, good and bad tactical decisions are made by the parties and, like a hard-fought historic battle, the ground is won and lost as the battle ebbs and flows.

As ever, the starting point for analysis has to be what the legal position might be. That is why it is important to ascertain first of all who owns what. If there really are assets that do not belong to the company but to individual shareholders, and if there is consensus, then resolution of that aspect of ownership is easy. There then would be left only the question of the shares and what is to happen to them. The legal rights to buy and sell shares *must* be clear before moving forward.

> *As with the analysis of who owns what, it isn't sensible to engage with the other shareholders until the legal rights and the processes of buying and selling shares is understood.*

The basic outcomes about what happens to the shares are obvious: either the shares of one or more shareholders are bought by other shareholders, or they are sold to an 'outsider', or the entire shareholding is sold, or the business closes. Of course, the parties might resolve their differences and find a way of continuing together. If that is not to be then any one of these scenarios is a dramatic shift in the dynamics of the business.

The usual outcome of a Business Divorce is that one party will buy out the other party's share interest so that the business continues; analogous to one party staying in the family home in a marital divorce. That outcome is best determined by negotiation. There are circumstances in which a court might become involved and determine the outcome of the shareholding (see Chapter 2-4) but it is very wrong to assume that the court will always be willing to intervene. In very many circumstances, there will simply not be the factual basis for intervention. Unlike many partnership situations where one or more of the partners have reached a point where they can no longer work together and are able to dissolve their partnership, shareholders generally are without that option. Unless there is provision in the articles or a shareholders' agreement to compel a sale or purchase of shares then the shareholders can be stuck with their shares and stuck with one another. That is when the situation and the relationship breaks down and parties are exposed to the risk of bad decisions that might influence a negotiated settlement or a court case.

> *The answer to situations where there is uncertainty as to who gets what must be for the parties to work hard, perhaps with the assistance of a facilitator, conciliator or a mediator, to reach a resolution and to do so quickly.*

Value

What is the business worth? What is a shareholding worth? Who is to decide this?

In the majority of cases, the dispute, the negotiation and the outcome will be focused upon the basic question – how much? The parties shouldn't wait to find this out by reading the report of an independent professional valuer appointed at the direction of the court as an expert or even appointed by agreement between the parties.

> *BIG TIP Anyone entering the dispute arena, whether they arrive before or after the whistle is blown to start play, needs to know what the probable values of the business and the relevant shareholding might be. Engage a professional valuer as soon as possible.*

> *Tip for lawyers: don't overlook O'Neill and another v Phillips 1992*

This doesn't mean that a party must commission a detailed valuation report of the kind that a court might expect an expert to prepare – although it is often very useful, if this is affordable. Without professional guidance, parties really will be exposed to the risk of wasting costs if the dispute turns litigious. They could also be embarrassed at a negotiation or mediation if they cannot demonstrate how they have calculated their figure for settlement. It is rarely good enough to simply say: "That's the figure I want!" Such statements are usually made by parties who think they have a solid position but haven't prepared and haven't researched the legal and factual reality.

There are different ways to value a business and the value of a shareholding in a business. The most popular are:

- a multiple of recurring earnings;
- net asset valuation;
- dividend yield; and
- break-up valuation.

The necessity to consider past and future financial

performance, to make appropriate adjustments and to consider taxation implications has to be for financial advisers to deal with. If it is possible for a party to engage an independent valuer who would be able to comply with the provisions of Rule 35 of the Civil Procedure Rules then so much the better, as the evidence from such an expert might be capable of use if the dispute comes to trial. Even so, a party usually establishes credibility in presenting an opinion from an independent professional. That can be useful in direct negotiation or at a mediation.

Shareholders should not be left mystified by a valuation. A shareholder may expect to hear the expression EBITDA, meaning Earnings Before Interest, Tax, Depreciation and Amortisation. It is just one way of measuring a company's earning potential. It is sometimes argued that EBITDA is overused as a performance measure, particularly where there is no significant loan liability.

> *Whatever valuation method may be recommended, the reason for using a particular method should be understood and accepted, or challenged.*

A further word of warning, however, is that sometimes valuers can be hasty in their consideration of discounting valuations for shareholdings, particularly for minority interests. Once written, the die is cast. Discounts can be as much a matter of legal judgment, particularly if relevant to the behaviour of the parties, as they might be a matter of commercial judgment relevant to a market sale. It should therefore be left for the parties and their negotiating team to deal with any discount.

> *Big Tip: Make it clear to any independent valuer that, at least in the first instance, they are not expected to consider any discounting of a shareholding interest.*

However, it isn't just about the money. Rarely are Business Divorce disputes easily or quickly resolved. The impact that a dispute can have upon personal well-being should never be underestimated or ignored, either by the parties involved or their advisers. There is also likely to be an impact upon the business itself, not least because of the distraction of time and energy by those involved.

Who Stays and Who Goes

If parties have reached a position where they are no longer able to continue to participate in business together but the business is to continue, how is it determined who stays and who goes?

Of course, it may be that one party has resolved to leave in any event, perhaps for health reasons or retirement. There may also be a simple position of only one party being able to afford to purchase the share interest of the outgoing party. If it is a case, however, that both or more than one of the shareholders wants to stay, battle lines are drawn.

Without there being a legal solution within the articles or the shareholders' agreement then commercial considerations are likely to prevail. Very often, articles or shareholders' agreements will provide a procedure for notice, counter notice, offer and counter offer. There may be provision for referral to a third party for determination of share price. Sometimes these procedures include a mechanism for flip-flop offers whereby an offer made by one party to purchase the shares of another can be reversed by the recipient of the offer, thus preventing the original offeror making an unfairly low initial offer. This solution method is sometimes adopted as an outcome to an arbitration process.

The commercial considerations are not simply financial. Realistically, who is likely to have the goodwill of the customer base? Would it be the finance director or the sales director? Is it the engineering director or the managing director who knows the technical issues and solutions of the production process?

> *Anticipate but don't presume who stays and who goes.*

However, what if the business is capable of division? How can the parties be comfortable about the evenness of the playing field going forward? Read on...

Protections and Restrictions

Whether one party is to buy the share interest of another or whether the parties have decided to go their separate ways with each continuing the same type of business, the parties will be wanting comfort that the deal they do and the price to be paid or received is worthwhile. Not only will that involve an assessment of the alternative costs and opportunities of a different resolution, probably it will involve a wish (perhaps a need) to protect the 'investment' to be made in the continuing or new business.

Restrictive covenants protecting a customer base and staff structures, along with express and implied duties of confidentiality, might already have been part of the negotiation process and determination of the sale price or settlement. The necessity for the continuation or introduction of restrictions and conditions could be equally as influential in the determination of price or settlement. The parties need to think about their commercial exposure and what really needs to be protected. These should be formulated and enunciated at the beginning of negotiations.

3 *From the beginning think of **Protecting the Settlement.***

- *Share vendors must think of the security of the payment agreed;*
- *Share purchasers must formulate and enunciate the requirement for protections and restrictions at the beginning of negotiations. Introducing them later in the process is usually less credible and less rewarding.*

Chapter 3-3: War and Peace

Reconciliation

Is it really at an end? The expression Business Divorce is poignant. Shared business ownership has similarities to marriage: the personal relationship is important; assets are commonly owned; there is an emotional as well as a real cost in breaking up and very often others are affected by it.

It is not the purpose of this notebook to deal with the merits and detriments of reconciliation but the reader is invited to weigh this as part of the overall consideration of the process and the pros and cons of going through a Business Divorce.

For shareholders there sometimes isn't an easy escape route. It rarely happens in marital divorces today that a married couple has to wait five years for a divorce on the basis of separation without consent. For shareholders who want out but don't have a legal grievance to insist upon a buy-out, their wait can be much longer. Sometimes there is a strategic advantage in deciding to wait, playing a long game and just being a thorn in the side of the other shareholders (see Chapter 4-1). Without a legal imperative to deal with the situation, there can be scope for one or more parties to exploit it.

> *All shareholders need to be prepared for time taking its toll commercially and personally. For these reasons alone, it is perhaps wise never to say never to reconciliation.*

Litigation

Prepare to fight!

Litigation is often the alternative to an amicable resolution. It brings with it the possibility of a slowly eroding shareholder relationship with acrimony or increased acrimony and perhaps with the risk of a decaying business. Unless there is a contractual obligation, or the parties agree to take a dispute to arbitration, the ultimate forum for a decision on who is right is the court. It is rare, however, for shareholder dispute cases to go to court and to the bitter end with a judge giving a judgment and awarding costs, because:

- The circumstances in which shareholders may have a 'cause' to bring a claim against other shareholders are limited (see Chapter 2-4);
- It would be dangerous to assume that, in 2018, a party to a contested shareholder dispute will spend less than £100,000 to take a dispute to trial. In many circumstances this will be a very conservative estimate;
- The losing party risks being ordered to pay the other side's costs;
- If presented as a claim with a monetary value, the court costs on issuing are now five per cent of the value of the claim between £10,000 and £200,000, and £10,000 above that top level;

- There is usually a significant level of uncertainty regarding the outcome of court proceedings.

For these reasons, the threat of litigation should not be overplayed. Nevertheless, parties must always remain alive to the possibility that settlement will not be achieved, and that litigation might follow. Along with that will come all of the tactics of litigation. If lawyers are involved with the dispute process then, even if the parties have agreed to talk or to mediate, it must be expected that, from the beginning, the lawyers will manoeuvre to protect their client from the dangers and risks of subsequent litigation.

The lawyers as well as the lay client need to know what prospects there may be of a successful outcome. "What are the chances of success?" is always a fair question for a client to ask. "It all depends" is nearly always a fair answer. What is important is that the lawyers and the client analyse and assess just what success depends upon. With that must come a good interrogation of relevant facts and a good understanding of the law. Clients mustn't hold back material information, lawyers must listen and both must be honest with the other about any lack of understanding. The expense of engaging an expert, perhaps a barrister (also known as counsel), at an early stage to provide advice or opinion can often be money well spent. An appreciation of the possible legal position is important in determining strategy and tactics (see Part Four).

In addition to the legal merits, the lawyers will be thinking about how to protect the position on costs and how this might be used as a lever in negotiation at the time or at some later time. Parties will by advised by their lawyers about offers to make and how to make them as a means of cost protection and leverage. (see Settlement, below).

Settlement

Prepare to settle!

The conclusion of reading this notebook will hopefully be that it is simply better to talk than it is to walk away; that it is better to mediate rather than to litigate; to jaw-jaw rather than war- war!

I anticipate that few business people will need persuasion on this or even need to get to the end of the notebook to reach this conclusion. A difficulty is how to get to the negotiation table without parties feeling that simply to do so is a weakness.

Most business people will have their own style of negotiation and will want to control the negotiation their way. My belief is that a valuable amount of energy is wasted worrying about what the other side will think if you suggest a meeting or if you make the first offer. Once the parties find the courage to talk neither of these points are of any consequence.

> *There is merit in appearing to be and being the reasonable party in a negotiation. Suggesting a meeting and looking to make the first offer often gives credibility to the position of the proposer.*

Whether discussions to settle or a mediation are promoted by the parties themselves, by the lawyers or at the direction of the court, here are a few terms which disputing parties need to understand and grasp:

Without Prejudice: any communication made by one party to the other and labelled to be without prejudice cannot be disclosed to the court. Thus, a without prejudice offer is an offer which will not be disclosed to the court; at least not before a judgment has been given.

Part 36: is a provision of the Civil Procedure Rules that deals with without prejudice offers made before or during the conduct of proceedings. Such offers have particular consequences for costs depending upon when they are made, the nature of the dispute and the outcome. The underlying principle is that a party who makes an offer before judgment is given, which is an offer better for the opponent than the judgment award itself, should enjoy a benefit when costs are considered. After all, time and money might have been saved all round if the offer had been accepted.

An Open Offer: is simply an offer that does not enjoy the protection of being kept a secret between the parties. It is an offer a judge could be told about before he makes his decision and so it could have an influence on how a judge sees the facts and determines the outcome.

Privilege: is how lawyers refer to communications that protect subsequent use or reference to information and communications which should not be disclosed, either to the other party or to the court. Thus, a without prejudice offer made by one party to the other is a privileged communication between the parties.

This really is the tactical lawyers' battlefield. The right offer made at the right time can turn or determine the outcome of a dispute. The courts have been increasingly encouraging of parties to settle disputes and part of that encouragement has been delivered by the development of the rules on costs consequences and costs orders. With the level of costs for a Business Divorce of the kind suggested above and with added consequences, this really is an aspect of negotiation and litigation that must be grasped.

Parties to a Business Divorce who do not engage lawyers still need to understand the fundamental distinction between open and without prejudice communications. Thought should be given not only to what is said and when it is said but also how it is said. If a party wants to disclose something they would not want a judge to know about, whether it be an admission of some kind or a generous offer, then the party should consider making the statement or offer on a without prejudice basis – perhaps it should only be made in writing which records, at the beginning, that it is made without prejudice. It is not so easy to preface a face to face conversation or a telephone call with the words "without prejudice" and there is unlikely to be hard evidence that the conversation is privileged.

This entire area isn't easy for lay people and sometimes not for the lawyers. Often the without prejudice heading is used when nothing privileged is written or said and a court might decide that, as there is no need for the protection of privilege, none shall attach to the statement. On other occasions, a court might find that the circumstances of communication between the parties was intended to be privileged and so rule that a statement should enjoy the label of it being 'without prejudice'. How confusing is that!

> *If you are unsure then play safe. If you want the opportunity to communicate on a without prejudice basis send a letter or an email to the other party stating that the forthcoming meeting or perhaps all subsequent communications are to be on a without prejudice basis.*

Part Four: Achieving the Objective

Chapter 4-1: Strategies

Having reviewed and understood the basics of the business and the dispute and having determined the objective, then is the time to determine a strategy. This involves some review of the previous analysis and perhaps of the objective itself, but most of all it requires realism and a large measure of reality testing.

> ༃ *Parties to a dispute should remain passionate about their position, do their best to put aside emotions and listen to the voices of reality within and around them.*

Have a Strategy!

All too often the enemies march towards one another without considering a strategy. They may have set an objective and there may have been a good measure of analysis and preparation but the method by which to achieve the objective is sometimes made up along the way.

Not to determine a strategy is the same as setting off on the journey where a destination (the objective) might have been determined (perhaps by someone else!) but without considering the best method to get there. Do you travel by train or go by car? You really cannot leave home without deciding the means by which you will travel and you shouldn't think of progressing a Business Divorce without thinking of the means by which you will achieve your objective.

Your objective might always stay the same but it rarely works to be inflexible with a strategy. If you have chosen to travel to Inverness from London by car but find that snow has closed the roads from Glasgow, you might want to travel by train for the rest of the journey. It is sensible to have a willingness to change a strategy in order to react correctly to changing circumstances. Pride should not get in the way of success and even the professional advisers need to be prepared to recommend a change of strategy if the current strategy isn't going to work.

> ☞ *Be realistic in setting the strategy. It may cost less to walk to Inverness but will you get there?*

The Good and the Bad

There is a danger in seeing the actions of the other party as bad and/or mischievous, believing that this would be relevant to a court of law and that somehow justice will prevail. That may be so, but it is a dangerous post to lean upon. The common attitude of any court will be to accept that a relationship has broken down and unless there are wrongdoings which will impact upon the decision the court has to make, bad behaviour may be irrelevant. That is not to say that it should be ignored or that it may not be relevant, particularly on issues such as costs, but it should not usually be relied upon as determining the outcome.

That is not comforting news to owners who feel they have

been wronged by the other party but if it can be accepted then a better focus may be achieved on a relevant and successful strategy and appropriate tactics.

> ☧ *Avoid being righteous: it's not always about rights and wrongs.*

Assessing and Understanding Respective Positions

In a Business Divorce, parties must grasp three key elements for there to be a successful outcome, whether by negotiation or other process: the real cause of the dispute, the legal merits of respective positions and the negotiating strengths of the parties.

The Real Cause of Dispute

Part Three dealt with the preparation required before the litigation or negotiation gets underway. That preparation should help a party in determining the real objective and what to expect in the process of either war or peace. It should also have assisted in providing a better understanding of the position of the other side. In litigation, if one party does not understand the other side's case or how it is put then, sometimes with the assistance of the court, steps can be taken to obtain clarification. If negotiation is to take place, it is still important for the parties to know the real position of the other side. In mediation this is usually achieved by the exchange of position statements before the mediation takes place. They will be exchanged on a without prejudice basis (see Chapter 3-3) and should allow parties to really say what their true grievance or position might be. Usually, the mediator still has to work at getting to the bottom of real issues. So often there are underlying causes of dispute which never surface. Whilst sometimes it is better if that remains so, it is difficult for parties to meet the real and reasonable expectations of the other side if underlying issues are not uncovered.

> *It is incumbent on a mediator to look beneath the surface and really understand the position of each party. Sensible parties to litigation and negotiation must do likewise.*

Legal Merits

As mentioned in Part Three, parties must understand the legal merits of their position and the prospects of success. That requires a reasoned assessment of how the other side will see its legal position.

In litigation the parties' positions should be discernible from pre-action letters before claim and response or from the pleadings (primarily the particulars of claim and defence). Of course, these documents only express how the parties want to present their positions. The task of the lawyers is to pick through the stated positions, to analyse, and to advise on the true merits of the positions. Often this can only be done when all the evidence is available as well. This might not be until after exchange of witness evidence, expert evidence, disclosure of documents and much money spent! So don't delay some evaluation of the merits. Any evaluation should be constantly reviewed and the earlier there is some view taken on merits then the easier it is to begin to determine a strategy. (See Chapter 4-4 and the notes on Neutral Evaluation.)

Evidence is more likely to change legal advice on merits and disclosure is therefore an important step in litigation. The parties often fear disclosure because they must disclose documents even if they are to the detriment of their case. Lawyers will be rightly precious in following this obligation and the client must take on board this concept of openness from the start. Not least, the client must be open and honest with advisers from the beginning. To be otherwise will not only risk undermining the relationship but also risks producing a misleading assessment of the legal merits. This principle applies whatever dispute resolution process is used.

> *An early reality check on the legal merits of a position can be a pre-requisite to a successful outcome.*

Negotiation Strengths

An analysis of respective negotiation strengths in a Business Divorce is, a little crudely, an analysis of the legal merits, the financial condition of the parties and an assessment of their attitude and commitment.

If the negotiating strength of one party is its financial superiority and if the negotiating weakness of the other party is its financial impoverishment then one might say that the respective legal merits become irrelevant, but that should not necessarily be so. What becomes important to the outcome is the attitude and commitment of the parties.

So often the situation is that the party with the strongest financial position is seeking to oust a weaker party who has a stronger legal position but not the financial wherewithal to do anything about it. Then the issue is often determined by who needs the Divorce most at that particular time, as well as the attitude and commitment to achieve that.

The weaker and perhaps intimidated parties often sense little hope of a successful outcome. The comfort can be that the oppression, bullying and prejudicial actions of the superior party may be to no avail if the weaker party is prepared to be patient and play a long game, and can afford to do so mentally.

> ℑ *Don't assume that the strongest financial position will win the day and don't underestimate the value of patience.*

Strategies for Leavers and Remainers

The Minority and Outgoing Shareholders (the 'Leavers')

As mentioned in Chapter 3-2 (Who Gets What), there must be an understanding of the rights to buy and sell shares. That is so whatever dispute, reason for change or grievance the minority or Leavers may have.

It is very often the minority who become disenchanted and want to leave. They must be mindful that the law will uphold the principle of majority rule unless there is something unjust, inequitable or prejudicial about the relationship. This is very technical. (See Chapter 2-4: Remedies at Law). Here is where an early reality check is essential:

- If a minority shareholder does have a potential legal position because of an unjust, inequitable or prejudicial position is there funding to take that position forward and/or to use it as a lever for a settlement?
- Is there a really good prospect of a successful outcome?
- If the legal position isn't strong, are there any other lawful levers of persuasion?
- And, if there are not, don't embark upon futile and expensive actions...
- Look to other resolution solutions, such as mediation, adjudication or arbitration, where provided for in governing documents such as the articles of association or shareholders' agreement.
- If there isn't a contractual obligation to follow such solutions, consider inviting the other shareholders to participate in such a process.
- And, if the majority play a hard, non-conciliatory position then the minority must ... be patient.

Sometimes, patience must be the strategy if a party is

without an immediate legal or commercial solution and this is very often the position for a weak minority shareholder. If that is the case, then the minority shareholder should think of a long-term solution and adopt a behaviour of proper but regular contact with and monitoring of the company/other shareholders, ensuring that the minority's share interest is never overlooked. If this is irritating to the majority, then it may provoke an earlier resolution.

The Majority and Remaining Shareholders (the 'Remainers')

In general, it might be expected that, subject to there *not* having been bad behaviour by the majority of the Remainers which might deprive them of a good legal position, they should hold the stronger ground, but again there needs to be an early reality check:

- What is the true relative financial strengths of the parties?
- What is the true cost of the dispute not being resolved quickly?
- Is there a legal weakness because of behaviour?
- What is the real assessment of the merits and the cost?

☽ *Whether a party leaves or remains, don't allow the other side to determine the process by their strategy unless it suits to do so. To counter a strategy, you must understand what it is, so spend time thinking deeply about what the other side are doing.*

Choosing a Strategy

What are the options? Usually there isn't any great sophistication and the choice may be determined by many factors, which may be personal and have little relevance to the art of warfare or negotiated peace.

Here are a few simple and obvious strategies:

- Formal and legal. The approach will be determined entirely by what the rules of the relationship and the law might be.
- Amicable and conciliatory. Whatever difficulties there might be, the parties will never become combatants.
- Determined, assertive and perhaps aggressive. An offended party might want to take control of the conduct and progress of the dispute to ensure the dispute gets resolved.
- Patient and pleasant. Usually adopted where there is belief that a 'long game' will produce the right result. In the meantime, nothing will be done to disturb the status quo.
- Patient but undermining. This can be employed when time might be on the side of one party, who will use tactics to frequently frustrate, damage and antagonise the other.

As considered above (see Negotiating Strengths), a party who is willing and capable of being patient and doing little *can be* in the strongest negotiating position. This is often the hardest strategy for an adviser to recommend and for a party to accept.

Do not ignore the strategic value of being as transparent as possible about facts, figures (valuations) and intentions. This not only appeals to the Business Divorce resolvers (judges, mediators and arbitrators), it is a very powerful aspect of a strategy which disarms opponents (see Chapter 2-3).

The strategies of opposing parties may conflict: early resolution against a 'long-play'; a conciliatory approach against a resolute approach; an expensive power-play against a weak or impoverished opponent. The strategy should not ignore what might be expected from the opponent, but it should not be entirely determined by it.

Determine your strategy but don't confuse strategies and tactics.

Chapter 4-2: Tactics

Introducing Tactics

If the objective of your journey is to reach Inverness (as we saw in Chapter 4-1) and your strategic decision was to travel by car then you should consider, as a matter of tactics, the route you are going to take. Of course, you can set off and just see how things go but a Business Divorce should not be a journey of serendipity.

This is not a chapter on *how to* litigate, mediate or negotiate. It will not, for example, instruct how to present a negotiation position of 'salami slicing' or 'blanketing' and it does not recommend how to plead particulars of claim in litigation. Aside from some general guidance on making and viewing offers, it is only intended to improve awareness of the opportunities and threats of tactics which have relevance to Business Divorce. The deployment and style of presentation of tactics must be determined by the objective, the strategy and the personalities of those involved.

Nevertheless, having determined a strategy, it is sensible to think ahead to what tactics (including offers) might be useful and when to employ them. Very often tactics emerge to suit a situation but some aforethought often avoids a spontaneous response to a situation that damages a planned tactical or strategic position.

> ☞ *Don't be tempted by an opportunity to employ a tactic that is inconsistent with the strategy.*

Winning an unnecessary skirmish doesn't win the war.

Advisers and Conflicts of Interests

Many shareholder disagreements will be resolved with the assistance of an adviser close to the business, usually the company external accountant. There is much sense in involving someone who knows the business and the parties involved but when the parties are to separate, more care is needed by the parties and the advisers.

Advisers commonly understand the importance of avoiding the embarrassment of a conflict of interest between the disputing parties. If it is possible for an adviser to smooth a misunderstanding between shareholders or to facilitate a debate between them then the outcome might justify the involvement. The Code of Ethics for the ICAEW and the Code of Conduct for solicitors indicate that to become involved could lead to a breach of the respective codes. Both codes contemplate circumstances where it might be appropriate for the professional to act or to continue acting for both parties but the issues of objectivity, confidentiality, awareness, benefits and risks are all factors the professionals and clients should consider and weigh up before the dispute process gets underway.

Surprisingly, a common error is for an adviser not to identify the client correctly. If an adviser is consulted by the Remainers, that does not mean that the adviser should be acting for the company as well as the Remainers. A

Business Divorce is not a battle with the company: it is between the shareholders. The company itself, as a legal entity, is usually peripheral to the dispute but if matters are not resolved and litigation does ensue then an adviser may be embarrassed if they have been purporting to act for the company as well as one or more of its shareholders. This might provide a tactical game-play position (see below, Other Traps, Tricks and Tips – Confidentiality). The problem usually manifests at an early stage, with the company being billed for the adviser's fees when they should be the responsibility of the individual shareholders.

> *In a Business Divorce dispute between shareholders the company should not pay the fees of advisers for individual shareholders.*

Offers

Within the process of dispute and resolution, there is little more that is 'tactical' than making an offer. Reference has already been made to open, without prejudice and Part 36 offers in Part Three, which dealt with Preparation (see Chapter 3-3: Settlement). It is a poor tactical position to enter into negotiation or to become involved in litigation without having thought about a settlement position.

First offers are usually regarded as starting a process of haggling, which, ultimately, gets to a middle ground area of settlement. Very often that is so. It is dangerous to believe that it is always so and particularly when Part 36 offers are made. Sometimes parties make offers to preserve a position, especially with regard to costs, and often it is difficult to move parties from those protective positions.

Thus, it can be dangerous to view a first offer, and perhaps subsequent offers, as just part of a step process towards settlement. Each offer should be viewed in isolation against the offeree's own wishes and needs.

However, it is equally as dangerous for parties to negotiate on the basis of final offers. Would a party pay or receive £1 less or £1 more to clinch a deal? The art of successful negotiation involves credibility and to make threats or to give ultimatums which are unrealistic, unachievable or unsustainable can damage a party's credibility and likely damage the outcome for that party.

A party making an offer should always have regard to how the offer will be received. If the offeror really wants to settle, then it is futile to make an offer if its only outcome is to inflame the attitude of the other side.

- *Respect and dignity in negotiation may be as valuable as the strength of the legal merits of a position.*

- *Remember always to try and understand how the other party sees things.*

The Legal Tools and Levers

Good preparation should identify the threats and

opportunities which could arise during the dispute process. Most commonly, these will arise as part of the continuing conduct and relationship of shareholders in business together rather than as traps and opportunities within a litigation or resolution process.

> *Usually every opportunity comes with a risk and that must be balanced in the decision-making process on tactics.*

Breaches and Wrongs

Simply being a shareholder imposes little responsibility. Being an employee or director as well as a shareholder of the company changes the position immensely. Directors and employees owe duties. Critically, those duties are owed to the company itself. There may be duties expressed within an employment contract or service agreement and there are statutory duties directors must observe as well as implied duties that both employees and directors cannot ignore (see Chapter 2-4).

This may seem like a minefield, but much is underpinned by common sense. It will be of no surprise that directors and employees, in broad terms, owe a duty of good faith to the company and that directors have a fiduciary duty to the company. Employment law and company law, both in common law and by statute, have developed legal principles which go beyond the scope and purpose of this notebook. The shareholder-employee or the shareholder-director, however, should forever be cautious of actions taken by themselves and cautious also of criticism of the actions of others.

The simple list of directors' duties which is now codified in sections 171-177 of the Companies Act 2006 is:

- To act within powers;
- To promote the success of the company;
- To exercise independent judgment;
- To avoid conflicts of interest;
- Not to accept benefits from third parties; and
- To declare interest in a proposed transaction or arrangement.

There is really nothing surprising within that list. What is surprising is the frequency with which the duties are flouted when it comes to managing relationships between shareholders in dispute. Depending on the outcome, one might judge the actions as brave or foolhardy. Bullying shareholder-directors will do what they like and challenge the other shareholders to do something about it.

1   If the disgruntled shareholders have the power at board level, they may be able to change or correct the consequence of the improper action;

2   If the disgruntled shareholders do not have board control but have control as shareholders, they may be able to deal with the situation in general meeting;

3   However, if they are a powerless minority, they must consider applying to the court for

permission to bring a derivative action in the name of the company (see Chapter 2-4); or

4   They use the improper action as grounds to petition for the winding up of the company under section 122 Insolvency Act 1986, or to present an unfair prejudice petition under section 994 Companies Act 2006 (see Remedies at Law in Chapter 2-4).

Probably none of these options will meet with much approval from affected shareholders who want to stay away from confrontation and, particularly, to stay away from any court action. Their reluctance or weakness to act will be to the advantage of the bullying or brave miscreant shareholder. Nevertheless, improper actions should not be allowed to pass without note. If the weak or the minority later have cause and the wherewithal to do something, then a recorded history of poor behaviour could be of real relevance.

> *The affected shareholders should seize every opportunity to protest and to record their protest even if they think it will have no immediate impact upon the miscreants.*

> *Do not engage in tit-for-tat impropriety, no matter how tempting it may be, as there is often still opportunity to use the improper behaviour as a lever in negotiation.*

Restrictions

Part of the preparation for the Business Divorce should have been to examine what protections and restrictions might exist in the various legal documents: the shareholders agreement, employment and service contracts. Post termination restraints might have a commercial value depending on the parties' intentions post-Divorce but *current* as well as post termination restraints very often have a tactical value during the Divorce process. While the process is underway, neither side should risk a contractual breach. This may not only allow the other side to win a skirmish but the skirmish itself could turn into an expensive and damaging battle.

> *Stay focused on the objective and avoid the risk of gifting an opportunity or advantage to the other side by breaching a restraint.*

Removals and Dismissals

If employees and/or directors do act wrongfully by failing in their duties or by breach of a restraint, then they may be exposed to removal or dismissal from their positions.

The removal of a director isn't simply within the gift of the managing director or the board of directors unless there is an express power already provided. The Companies Act requires a process to be followed for the removal of a director by the shareholders by ordinary resolution and entitles the director to a right to protest (s168 and s169

Companies Act 2006). Be aware that the removal itself doesn't deprive a director of any compensation or damages that might be payable.

It is very often overlooked that a participating shareholder is usually employed by the company. A shareholder-employee will have the same employment protection rights as other employees. When something goes wrong and the shareholder-employee is *excluded* from the business, there is often the opportunity for the excluded shareholder-employee to claim an unfair dismissal. When it comes to subsequent negotiation on the Business Divorce settlement, this can be a significant legal and commercial lever. It also affords the excluded shareholder-employee the control of the timetable as the process to pursue the unfair dismissal claim before an Employment Tribunal could dictate the timetable for a comprehensive settlement negotiation.

> *Avoid over-excitement when a shareholder-director or shareholder-employee does something wrong. Don't begin a removal process unless it really is a step towards the objective. Skirmishes of this kind are usually expensive in time and costs.*

Termination and Dissolution

As part of understanding the business, the parties should have examined any shareholders' agreement for a provision to manage share buy-outs (or to close the business) in defined circumstances by a defined process (see Chapters 1-2 and 4-4).

Does the business have to continue because of share buy-out provisions? Although it might make good commercial sense for it to do so, who is going to get the commercial benefit of this? It may be that it is fair for the business to be sold or closed. If so, the legal remedies available under s994 Companies Act 2006 (Unfair Prejudice) and s122 Insolvency Act 1986 (Just and Equitable Winding Up) should be considered for their legal leverage value as a threat to close the business if a settlement cannot be achieved.

Procedural Tactics

The parties to the Business Divorce and even advisers involved might not like it, but the reality is that the legal procedure of the Divorce will give rise at various times to tactical opportunities. For example, disclosure obligations during litigation or arbitration processes are fertile for parties to tease, to embarrass, to delay and, of course, to increase the expense of the Business Divorce. In recent years, cost budgeting itself has become a tactic in the weaponry of the lawyers to intimidate the opposition.

However, even the seemingly less aggressive process of mediation affords opportunity for tactical game-play. The very step of mediation itself can now sadly be used to increase costs and delay resolution when there is no genuine intention to use mediation for settlement.

For these reasons, parties should give more thought to the appropriate process to resolve a Business Divorce, if not at the time of starting business or in a shareholders' agreement then at least before any process gets underway. (See Chapter 4-4: Solution Vehicles.)

> *It is usually better for the parties to have control over the process than to allow the process itself to determine the path and progress of resolution.*

Other Traps, Tricks and Tips

Majority Rule

The value of the principle of majority rule is worth repeating. Although the power must be used properly and, at times of dispute, carefully to avoid challenges of oppression and unfair prejudice, it remains fundamental to the conduct of company business. To that extent it may still be used by the majority to achieve their will so it can be considered as a tool of persuasion in settlement negotiations.

Guarantees

A common commercial weakness might be the existence of personal guarantees having been given by only one of the disputing parties. Any real exposure should be covered by the guarantor before the process begins to avoid the weakness being exploited during negotiation. Could there be a right of contribution from co-shareholders? The legal position and the reality of the financial position should have been examined beforehand – by both sides to the dispute.

Loan Accounts

Similarly, where directors have loan accounts the liability of the director to the company or vice versa, as well as the lawfulness of the loan, must be understood before any Business Divorce process begins. Unlike the value of a shareholding, the amount of a loan account should not be a matter of negotiation but the requirement and the ability to pay or repay an account may be an influence on negotiating positions.

Company Audit

The provision in s476 Companies Act 2006 can be exceptionally useful to a minority shareholder faced with a majority who may wish to avoid an audit of the company's financial affairs. It is a right available to members of a company representing not less than ten per cent (in nominal value) of the company's issued share capital to require a company to obtain an audit when it would otherwise be exempt from doing so. Thus, it only applies to 'small companies' as they are statutorily defined, but this covers most businesses where a Business Divorce is likely to happen.

The timing of the notice requesting an audit is important. It must be given not later than one month before the end of the relevant year but cannot be given before that year begins. The party giving the notice should be mindful that a consequence will be an additional cost to the company.

Resignation as a Director

The removal of shareholders who are directors and/or employees is dealt with above under Legal Tools and Levers. Whatever opportunity there may be in the ability of one party to remove another, there will be a counter-risk and that must be balanced in the decision process on tactics. The same is true of a shareholder choosing to resign as a director. What is the value of a shareholder-director resigning if he/she then loses access to company information? What is the value in staying a director if the shareholder is then exposed to personal financial risk because of the way in which business is carried out?

The decision may be as much influenced by commercial considerations. If a shareholder expects to be departing the business and starting a fresh business elsewhere then it might be wise to remain involved and to maintain contacts with customers and suppliers. It may also be an encouragement to the other party to agree settlement terms.

Employees

The position as an employee is different. Little benefit is gained by leaving employment voluntarily unless there is somewhere better to move to. Often it is difficult for someone to remain involved, particularly if the shareholder is a persecuted minority. From one perspective the shareholder should be considering the position in pure employment terms. If the shareholder, as an employee, is being treated wrongfully then, with legal advice, there should be consideration as to whether there could be a constructive dismissal entitling the shareholder-employee to compensation.

This needs to be considered also by the other party to avoid gifting such a position and argument to the outgoing shareholder-employee.

Dividends

If dividends are commonly or regularly paid – and particularly if they are treated as part of the 'remuneration' package of a participating shareholder – then the timing and amount of such dividends should not be ignored, either in any formal proceedings or in any negotiation.

They should also not be overlooked by any paying party. It could be frustrating for either party to agree terms of settlement and for the question of dividends due *or overpaid* to be raised as an additional item.

Confidentiality

As mentioned previously, professional advisers need to be careful in conflict of interest situations. The adviser who has been paid by the company for advice given to only one side of the Business Divorce may inadvertently open the door for the other side to demand disclosure of that advice on the basis it has been provided to the company and not to individual shareholders. This is linked to the right of shareholders to company information and the different entitlement between shareholders and shareholders who are also directors.

> *Tactics should be used to help achieve the objective, not to irritate the other side. Such use of tactics is rarely effective.*

Chapter 4-3: Practical Problems and Solutions

Costs

It is fundamental that all involved have an early appreciation of the likely cost of a Business Divorce. No one really needs warning that taking any dispute to court is expensive but even if an alternative dispute resolution process is used or even if the parties negotiate direct and without advisers, there will be consequential costs which include the time, opportunity costs and impact on personal health and wellbeing as well as the monetary cost. The parties involved should not ignore consideration of costs even if lawyers are not involved or seem not to be involved at the start.

It is difficult even for the lawyers at the start of a dispute to commit to what the legal costs could be. Nevertheless, they must provide some guidance and estimate for the client. The key points for the lawyer and client to grasp at the start are:

- Is there a risk of or a need for urgent court action and, if so, what is the likely cost?
- How can the risk or the need for action be minimised?
- Is there proportionality between the possible costs and the value involved?
- Is there third-party funding/insurance available to assist with costs?

In many cases costs can be contained by the early intervention of lawyers for both sides and agreement on enforceable undertakings, a stay of any threatened proceedings, and agreement on procedures for early resolution.

Budgeting is all-important. In the litigation process, the courts will now want to see and approve budgets from all parties. The courts may also decide to cap the costs to be incurred to make them proportionate to the value of the dispute. At present it seems that the courts are more minded to control budgets rather than to cap costs.

The key point is that, in litigation, the parties have little control of the costs expenditure, whereas in arbitration, the parties may agree not only the amount of costs which might be awarded by the arbitrator but whether the costs incurred are recoverable at all by the successful party to the dispute. An arbitrator may also decide to cap costs. At the conclusion, unless the parties agree otherwise, the arbitrator will make a costs award similar to the way a court would do so. That is that costs will 'follow the event' – the successful party shall recover costs from the losing party, subject to assessment of reasonableness.

Funding the dispute process is often a hardship for one or more of the parties involved and this frustrates the progress of the process and often influences the outcome itself. This may be reason itself for a court or an arbitrator capping costs, but it remains the responsibility of the parties to manage the funding of their case. As mentioned above (Chapter 4-2: Advisers and Conflicts of Interest), the company itself should not be involved in funding a Business

Divorce between its shareholders.

> ༪ *The recoverability and the profile of costs expenditure should be understood at the beginning and should be reviewed regularly. Costs should be uppermost in mind when determining the objective, the strategy and the tactics.*

Taxation

Parties and their advisers frequently overlook the incidence of tax on settlement. At the least, before negotiations or a formal dispute process begins, the parties should take advice on the implications of possible outcomes. This is valuable in helping parties set parameters for acceptable settlement in negotiations (including mediation) and, in itself, this might promote settlement.

> ༪ *Don't treat taxation as irrelevant or incidental.*

Share Buy-back

When an outcome is reached whereby one party is to buy out the share interest of another, it is common for the purchase to be dealt with by a company buy-back of the shares. Regrettably, this is often raised only at the time of settlement or after terms have been agreed or a judgment delivered by a court or arbitrator.

HMRC's treatment of the taxation of the buy-back will

depend on rules which include consideration of the distributable reserves of the company, the period the shares have been held and the purpose of the buy-back. Taxation advisers will often recommend obtaining HMRC clearance for the company buy-back. Presenting this late in the negotiation process sometimes antagonises the parties and may frustrate the prospects of settlement. The buy-back process itself will require a buy-back agreement and shareholder approval requiring the co-operation of all the parties.

> *It is wise for the parties and their advisers to exchange thoughts early in the Business Divorce process on the prospects of a company buy-back and the timetable for dealing with it.*

Disposal of the Company

An agreed solution to the Business Divorce might be a sale of the business or a closure of the business and a sale of its assets. An agreement of this kind requires much care in the consideration and drafting of the terms because of the risks and opportunities there are for parties to behave poorly, which may damage the business and/or endanger the prospects of sale. The agreement needs to be tight in binding the commitment of all shareholders, not simply those at the heart of the Business Divorce.

> *If there is any element of mistrust or disagreement between business owners or any prospect of such*

then this is top of the list of circumstances in which the parties should seek separate independent advice and ensure that an agreement to sell is in place before any further steps are taken in the Business Divorce process.

Business Migration

The prospect of one party moving custom away from the business is a risk considered in Chapter 2-4 as part of the interim remedies which might be sought to protect the business. It is far better that the parties address this risk at the very beginning of the Business Divorce, even if the business protections are already in place in the form of employment and service contracts and a shareholders' agreement.

It may seem to be commercial naivety for a party who intends to depart and set up a rival business to have an open discussion about this, but it is more difficult for a company or the remaining shareholders to persuade a court of the need for protection if the leaving shareholders are open about their position.

> *Openness can avoid expensive litigation diversions.*

Chapter 4-4: Solution Vehicles

Defined Processes

The articles of association of a company will provide some rules for the transfer of shares and may provide for pre-emption rights in favour of existing shareholders. There may also be 'tag along' and 'drag along' rights to cover the rights where shares may be sold to a third party, usually as a takeover or merger arrangement. Whether seemingly relevant or not for the conduct and resolution of a Business Divorce, the articles must not be overlooked.

A shareholders' agreement may provide for a dispute resolution process and/or may have a process for the sale and purchase of shares. Thus, an agreement might require the parties to attend mediation or to proceed by way of arbitration or have a process to value the worth of shares in a company. That may involve the appointment of an expert (often the company's auditors) to value a shareholding. Sometimes more imaginative processes appear in shareholder agreements to help determine share values:

Russian Roulette: Where one party offers to buy the shares of another at a specified price for a limited period, or to buy the offeror's shares for the same price. If the offeree does not respond within the specified time, the offeree is deemed to have accepted the offer to buy his/her shares.

Mexican or Texan Shoot-out: Where one party offers the shares of another at a specified price. The offeree may then agree to sell at the offeror's price or offer to buy the offeror's shares at an unspecified higher price. Both parties then make sealed bids or enter into an auction.

Both processes have limitations and are more suitable for situations where there are just two shareholders. They are solutions, however, which are designed to achieve a fair result and may be used to significantly reduce the time and cost of Business Divorce. They may also avoid the acrimony which often accompanies or develops during a Business Divorce.

The content and enforceability of provisions in the articles may be more complicated in law but remember that the shareholders' agreement is the contractual arrangement between the shareholders and is therefore directly enforceable against other shareholders. The parties might agree to proceed with matters in a way different to a shareholders' agreement but if they choose to proceed differently to the provisions of the articles then formalities to amend the articles must be followed.

> *Do not overlook or ignore basic rules and provisions. This can be fatal. It may be that an existing defined process will provide a solution, and remember the parties can always **agree** to follow a different process.*

Litigation

In short, if the parties seek the best possible legally correct solution to their Business Divorce and costs and time are secondary issues then litigation is the process to follow. It is usual for one party to instigate the process, but the parties can agree that the courts should decide the dispute. Once started, however, the process will be managed by the courts. That isn't necessarily to the parties' detriment but the progress to trial is subject to the speed and efficiency of the courts as well as the parties.

It is also fundamental that the parties have a dispute which the court can rule upon. If the parties simply disagree on a share sale price without there being any underlying cause of action then the courts cannot help.

On the other hand, if the business itself or one party's interest is at risk because of the wrongful behaviour of the other, the courts are likely to provide the most effective interim solution to preserve the status quo.

Alternative Dispute Resolution

This expression loosely covers all solution vehicles other than litigation. Most common and most popular are mediation and arbitration but others which could be of relevance to Business Divorce include conciliation, neutral evaluation and expert determination.

Arbitration

Section 1 of The Arbitration Act 1996 provides that the "object of arbitration is to obtain a fair resolution of disputes by an impartial tribunal without unnecessary delay and expense" and it continues that "the parties should be free to agree how their disputes are resolved, subject only to such safeguards as are necessary in the public interest".

Some shareholders' agreements will provide for dispute resolution by arbitration and may identify the arbitrator or the organisation to be approached for the appointment of an arbitrator. Without such a provision, the parties may still agree to the appointment of an arbitrator.

A chapter could be written on the merits and disadvantages of arbitration but essentially the merits lie in section 1 of the Act: avoiding delay and expense, along with the freedom to agree the process. The disadvantages are often associated with the performance of the participants: an arbitrator who may not be impartial or who is unsuitable for the particular nature of the dispute; the over-zealous or the incompetent professional advisers who miss the point about achieving an efficient resolution which might still be 'fair'; the parties whose expectations of the fullest inquiry and most definitive ruling defeat the principles of achieving a fair result without unnecessary delay and expense.

Although arbitration is comparatively little used in Business Divorce, it might be more suitable in more cases than litigation if all participants get to grips with the proportionality of a fair result, time and cost.

Mediation

Mediation may be briefly explained as a private and non-binding form of dispute resolution in which the mediator, as a neutral participator, facilitates the parties to reach their own settlement of the dispute. To enable the parties to negotiate freely, the process provides for the mediation to be conducted on the basis of absolute confidentiality of all information disclosed during the mediation, that such information is privileged and that it cannot be used in subsequent proceedings.

Mediation is now an expected part of the litigation process and parties may expect the courts to require them to participate in mediation before the litigation process consumes all of the costs. That being so, the parties might consider mediation before any litigation commences. If it is unsuccessful, the parties may have another attempt at mediation further along the line.

If the mediator is adequately skilled *and* the parties are willing to compromise and sincere about wanting to settle, mediation can be a successful process.

Med-Arb

For the reasons indicated above, mediation may not work and yet in many cases it becomes impossible for one or both parties to bring the Business Divorce to a conclusion. The costs of carrying on litigation may be impossible to find or the lawyers may be nervous in advising that there are sufficient merits to do so. Yet for the parties it continues to be as difficult to carry on in business together as it is not to do so.

Sometimes there may be merit in asking the mediator to continue to act as an arbitrator and to determine the dispute between the parties. Hence the expression 'med-arb'. If the lawyers were nervous about proceeding with litigation, they should be as nervous about the outcome of an arbitration. Nevertheless, an arbitration following unsuccessful mediation could lead to a clean break Business Divorce, which might be cheaper and with an earlier determination than litigation might provide.

Conciliation and Expert Determination

Both offer short but, to some extent, incomplete solutions. A conciliator (as a competent independent third party) might succeed in bringing the parties together but they still have to work out the solution. Expert determination is often used for a single purpose, such as determining the value of the business (see Chapter 3-1).

Neutral Evaluation

I am a big supporter of this alternative dispute resolution process. It is often known as 'early' neutral evaluation because of the sensible use of it early in the dispute process before excessive time, energy and money are wasted.

It does what it says: an independent neutral person is appointed to evaluate either the whole dispute or particular issues. It makes sense to appoint someone knowledgeable in the subject matter. The evaluation will be non-binding on the parties, but it gives valuable guidance on whether the dispute should be continued. It can be particularly useful when the parties have diametrically opposed views.

The parties are still left to resolve matters but after a neutral evaluation the parties may find it easier to negotiate direct, or their choice of a suitable solution vehicle may be clearer:

- If the evaluation indicates that there are deeper matters to be explored without any obviously clear outcome, an adversarial process such as litigation or arbitration might be the choice.
- If the evaluation suggests that the outcome could go either way or that the differences between the parties are marginal or that both parties face disproportionate risks on costs and benefit, mediation would be sensible.

There is a danger that the evaluator gets it wrong and misleads the parties about the probable outcome. The choice of evaluator is, therefore, important. The real advantage, however, is the parties still have a choice and remain in control of settlement prospects as well as their participation in another resolution process.

> *If shareholders have reached a position where there is*
>
>> o *An issue between them which is seemingly unbridgeable; or*
>> o *an irretrievable breakdown in their relationship such that they can no longer be together as business owners;*

then they and their advisers should explore all possible processes for resolution and not simply engage in litigation.

Part Five: The Final Tips

Follow the structure of this Notebook:

- Understand the business and the dispute
- Set a realistic objective
- Have a strategy
- Identify relevant and effective tactics
- Use a suitable resolution process

About the Author

<u>Clive Tant</u>

Clive has been engaged with business structures since his undergraduate studies of accountancy and economics. As a business owner and practising solicitor, Clive has been committed to supporting local businesses and has chaired and held directorships of the local Chamber of Trade, Basildon Business Group and the local Enterprise Agency. He acted for several years as a judge for the Institute of Chartered Accountants in Essex Business Awards and has presented various seminars on legal and business issues.

He was a founder partner of Palmers Solicitors in 1983 and throughout his legal career he practised in commercial litigation, dealing with many high value claims of various kinds. More recently, with a growing reputation as a Business Divorce lawyer, he has concentrated on disputes between business owners.

Since 2010, Clive has been listed consistently in the Legal 500 and attributed with having *"the ability to see beyond the technicalities to predict the outcome..."* and as being *"very experienced and perceptive."*

Clive has been an accredited mediator and a member of the Chartered Institute of Arbitrators since 2006. Although Clive remains on the Roll of Solicitors, he is now non-practising and concentrates on his mediation and arbitration practice – with occasional book writing.

Made in the USA
Columbia, SC
02 March 2018